SPORTS CARS

IAN GRAHAM

Heinemann
LIBRARY

www.heinemann.co.uk/library

Visit our website to find out more information about **Heinemann Library** books.

To order:

☎ Phone 44 (0) 1865 888066

▤ Send a fax to 44 (0) 1865 314091

▢ Visit the Heinemann Bookshop at www.heinemann.co.uk/library to browse our catalogue and order online.

First published in Great Britain by Heinemann Library, Halley Court, Jordan Hill, Oxford OX2 8EJ, part of Harcourt Education.
Heinemann is a registered trademark of Harcourt Education Ltd.

Editorial: Dan Nunn
Design: Jo Hinton-Malivoire and Tinstar Design Limited (www.tinstar.co.uk)
Illustrations: Geoff Ward
Picture Research: Rebecca Sodergren and Bob Battersby
Production: Viv Hichens
Originated by Dot Gradations Ltd
Printed and bound in China by South China Printing Company

ISBN 0 431 16563 7 (hardback)
07 06 05 04 03
10 9 8 7 6 5 4 3 2 1

British Library Cataloguing in Publication Data
Graham, Ian, 1953–
    Sports cars. – (Designed for success)
    1. Sports cars – Juvenile literature
    I. Title
    629.2'221
A full catalogue record for this book is available from the British Library.

Acknowledgements
The publishers would like to thank the following for permission to reproduce photographs:
Alvey and Towers pp. **1**, **4**, **5** (bottom), **21** (top), **28**; Ariel Motor Company p. **27** (bottom); Auto Express pp. **7** (bottom x 3), **13** (top), **15** (top), **15** (bottom), **16**, **18**, **22**, **23** (top), **23** (bottom), **25** (bottom), **26**, **27** (top), **29**; Auto Express/Phil Talbot p. **5** (top); Car Photo Library/Dave Kimber pp. **3**, **6**, **11** (bottom), **12**, **13** (bottom), **20** (bottom), **21** (bottom), **25** (top); Colin Curwood p. **11** (top); Corbis pp. **9** (top), **24** (top); EPA p. **19** (top); Eye Ubiquitous p. **24** (bottom); Eye Ubiquitous/Darren Maybury pp. **8**, **9** (bottom); Eye Ubiquitous/Darren Maybury/McLaren p. **10**; Lotus p. **7** (top); McLaren p. **14**; TRH Pictures p. **17** (top).

Cover photograph reproduced with permission of Car Photo Library.

CONTENTS

Any words appearing in the text in bold, **like this**, are explained in the Glossary.

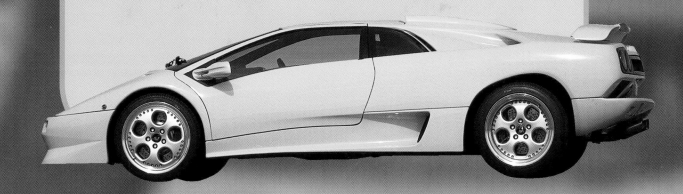

SPORTS CARS

A car's design reflects the way it will be used. Some cars are designed to carry a whole family and their luggage. Others are designed for making short trips in busy city streets. Sports cars are high-**performance** cars that are designed to be fun to drive.

Most sports cars are designed as high-performance road cars. A few of them are more like racing cars that have been redesigned for use on public roads. The most powerful sports cars are often called 'muscle cars'. The most expensive are called supercars. Supercars are so expensive because they use the best materials and technology. There are no sharp divisions between these different types of high-performance cars. A powerful supercar might also be a muscle car.

SUPER CAR

The Ferrari F50 is one of the fastest, most powerful and most expensive cars in the world. It is almost a racing car for the road. Its engine was developed from a **Formula 1** racing-car engine. Inside, it is quite bare, just like a racing car. The F50 is a very high-performance sports car for super-rich drivers.

COBRA POWER

One of the most famous sports cars was produced when an American ex-racing driver, Carroll Shelby, redesigned a British sports car, the AC Ace, and created the AC Cobra. It was a great road car and was also successful in motor racing. Its 4.7-litre **V8** engine gave it a top speed of up to 225 kmph (140 mph). Later versions had larger engines, up to 7 litres, giving them a top speed of 265 kmph (165 mph). The Cobra was so successful that **replicas** of them can still be bought in kit form for people to build for themselves.

FUN ON WHEELS

The German BMW Z3 is a typical modern sports car. It's a great-looking, open-top two-seater. It can be powered by a range of different engines to suit the performance that different drivers want.

BMW Z3

Engine size: 3.0-litre serial 6
Engine power: 230 hp
Length: 4.05 metres
Weight: 1360 kg
Top speed: 240 kmph (150 mph)
Seats: 2

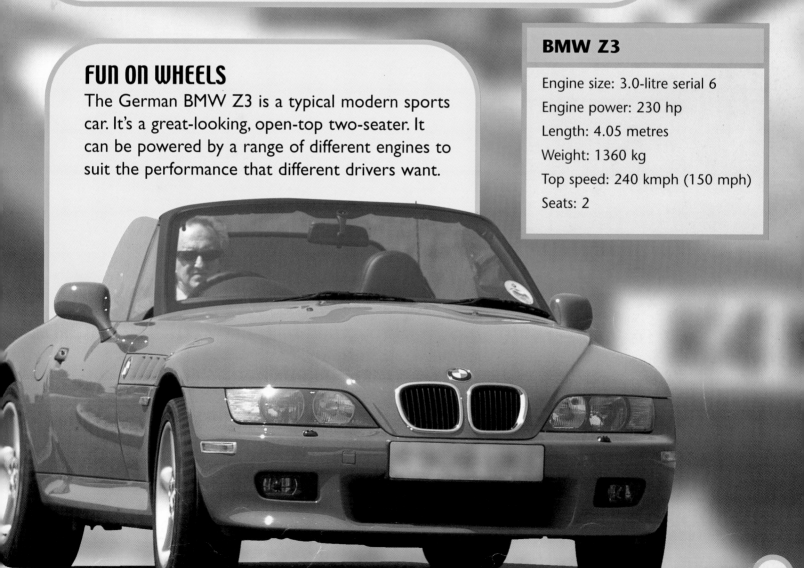

DESIGN FOR SPORT

A sports car's size, shape, weight and engine power are chosen by its designer to give the car the nimble **performance** that sports cars are known for.

The size and shape of a sports car are very important. A small, lightweight car is more **manoeuvrable** than a big, heavy car. So, most sports cars are small and lightly built. There is often enough room inside for only a driver and one passenger. A sports car also has to be the right shape to slip through the air quickly. That is why most sports cars have a low-slung body sitting close to the ground. It has to look sporty and exciting too. A smooth, gently curving body looks good and also lets air slide easily over the car. In many ways, the car's shape and design is decided by the performance it has to deliver.

BEST-SELLER
The Mazda MX-5 is the world's best-selling sports car. It has the layout of a classic sports car. It is a small, open-top two-seater. It has an engine mounted at the front of the car, driving the rear wheels. All sports cars used to be built like this, because it is a good way to achieve the performance and handling necessary for a sports car.

DRIVING A LIGHTWEIGHT

The Lotus Elise can out-perform many sports cars with bigger and more powerful engines. The key to its success is its ultra-light weight. Its **chassis**, or frame, is made from **aluminium**, and its body is made from a material called **GRP** (Glass Reinforced Plastic). The whole car weighs only 755 kilograms. That's about half the weight of many high-performance cars. Its extreme lightness means that it can obtain racing-car performance from a smaller engine. The Elise is powered by a 1.8-litre, 122-**horsepower** engine.

OPEN TO THE AIR

Even more fun than a sports car is an open-top sports car. Some sports cars have a fixed metal roof that can't be taken off. They're called fixed-head cars. Some have a detachable solid roof. Others have a roof made from soft material that folds away behind the seats. The Mercedes-Benz SLK is different. It has a solid roof that can fold like a soft roof at the flick of a switch. Within 30 seconds, the boot opens, the roof and rear window fold back out of sight and the boot closes again.

Merecedes-Benz SLK 32 AMG

Engine size: 3.2 litre V6
Engine power: 354 hp
Length: 4 metres
Weight: 1495 kg
Top speed: 250 kmph (155 mph)
Seats: 2

TRACK CARS

The designers who create racing sports cars use every trick of technology and materials available to produce the fastest cars.

They often make use of parts and materials developed for other vehicles. For example, the **disc brakes** that slow racing cars down were originally developed for aircraft. Eventually, new technology that proves its worth on the racetrack is built into new road-going sports cars. Racing sports cars are light, powerful and **streamlined**, just as road cars are. However, racing sports cars are even lighter, even more powerful and even more streamlined than road-going sports cars. Racing sports cars also need an extra-strong **chassis**, or frame, to stand up to super-fast cornering without bending or twisting. To save weight, some of the parts that are usually made from steel are replaced by parts made from lighter materials. **Aluminium** and **carbon fibre** are often chosen.

DAY AND NIGHT AT THE WHEEL

Most motor races last up to about three hours, but the world-famous Le Mans sports car race lasts for 24 hours. Each of the specially designed cars is driven by a team of drivers who each take turns at the wheel. The fastest Le Mans sports cars can reach 350 kmph (220 mph) on the fastest parts of the French racing circuit.

Chrysler Le Mans racing sports car

Engine size: 6.0-litre V8

Engine power: 585 hp

Length: 4.65 metres

Weight: 900 kg

Top speed: 350 kmph (220 mph)

Seats: 1

CARS WITH A WING

Racing sports cars often have a wing at the back. It works in the opposite way to an aircraft wing. As it cuts through the air, it pushes the car downwards. The faster the car goes, the more of this '**downforce**' the wing produces, pushing the car down more and more. This lets the car go round bends faster, because the tyres grip the track better.

wing

SPEEDY REPAIRS

Racing sports cars are designed to be taken apart very quickly. They may need to have damaged parts replaced. The nose and tail of the cars are usually detachable so that new ones can be fitted in a few seconds. During a long race, a car will probably also have its tyres replaced at least once. This is done by changing the entire wheels of the car. A road car's wheels are each held in place by four or five nuts and bolts. A racing sports car's wheels are usually held on by one big nut. It can be spun off using a power tool and the wheel pulled off and replaced within a couple of seconds.

This Porsche 911 GT1-98 is having its wheels changed during a pit stop.

MCLAREN F1
THE DESIGN FORMULA

The McLaren F1 is the world's most advanced sports car. It was designed by the same team that produces McLaren **Formula 1** racing cars.

The aim was to design the ultimate sports car using methods and materials from Formula 1 racing. It was important to make the car as light as possible, because lightweight cars **accelerate** faster than heavy cars. Another way to boost acceleration is to use a more powerful engine. The F1 is powered by a 600-**horsepower** engine made specially for the F1 by BMW Motorsport. For a sports car that can accelerate as fast as a racing car and reach a top speed of 386 kmph (240 mph), the shape of its body is very important. The wrong shape could slow the car down. The F1's body is designed to let air flow around it as smoothly as possible. Every detail of the car was designed to be the best possible shape, weight and strength.

POWERPLANT

The McLaren F1's engine is a 6.1-litre **V12** built with racing engine know-how. It's the smallest and lightest V12 ever built for a **production car**. It's about six times more powerful than the engine of a family car the same weight as the F1. The main part of the engine, called the engine block, is made from **aluminium** instead of steel to save weight.

The McLaren F1 engine (pictured left) is controlled by a computer ten times more powerful than the computers used in most family cars.

STAYING ON THE LEVEL

When an F1 driver brakes, a strip called a **spoiler** at the back of the car tilts up. Air rushing over the top of the car hits the spoiler and pushes the back of the car downwards. This **downforce** gives the rear wheels more grip so that they can slow the car down without skidding. The spoiler also helps to stop something called 'diving'. Most cars dip, or dive, at the front when they brake hard. The F1's spoiler pushes the back end of the car down, keeping the car level.

TUNNEL TESTS

The shape of the F1 was tested in a **wind tunnel**. As air was blown through the tunnel, the air pressure was measured at lots of points all over the car's body. To give an even better picture of how air flowed over the car, it was given a thick coat of paint that glows in the dark. The blowing air made the wet paint run and spread. It moved furthest where the air flowed fastest.

The McLaren F1's doors are designed to open upwards and outwards.

11

MCLAREN F1
HAND-BUILT IN CARBON FIBRE

Sports cars are usually made mostly from steel, but there are other materials that are lighter and stronger than steel, for example **carbon fibre**.

Most of the F1 is made from carbon fibre. In fact, the McLaren F1 is the world's first all-carbon-fibre road car. Most sports cars are mass-produced – they are built in large numbers on production lines. The F1 was built in much smaller numbers and each car was built by hand. When construction was complete, the car's body was painted with a special water-based paint. It was chosen because it is kinder to the environment than the oil-based paints that are normally used. The car has two onboard computers. One controls the engine to make sure it always works at peak **performance**. The second computer controls all the other electronic systems. It even detects when the car is doing more than 210 kmph (130 mph) and locks the windows so they can't be opened.

A METAL OVERCOAT

The McLaren F1's windscreen is covered by a metal coating so thin that it's see-through. This metallic film tints the screen, but it's not there to look pretty. It is designed to do an important job. An electric current passes through the metal layer, heating it up and gently warming the glass windscreen. The warmth keeps the screen free of mist and perfectly clear.

WHEEL DEALS

The McLaren F1's rear tyres are bigger than its front tyres. Most road cars have wheels and tyres that are all the same size. **Formula 1** racing cars have bigger rear tyres. This is because the rear wheels are driven by the engine. Big, wide tyres grip the ground better than small, thin tyres, so the car can accelerate without skidding. The McLaren F1 has bigger rear tyres for the same reason.

DUAL PURPOSE

Exhaust gases leave the engine through four big silencers. Their main job is to make the engine quieter. But the designers have cleverly given them a second job that makes the car safer. In an accident, the silencers are designed to soak up some of the impact, by being crushed. This will help to protect the people inside the passenger compartment.

silencers

MCLAREN F1
SIMPLY FAST

The McLaren F1 can out-perform every other car on the road. Its combination of **acceleration**, speed and **road-holding** are unmatched even by some racing cars.

From a standing start, the McLaren F1 can reach 100 kmph (60 mph) in just over 3 seconds. A typical family car would take about 10 seconds to reach the same speed. By then, the F1 could be doing more than 200 kmph (125 mph). This is about as fast as most family cars can go, but the F1 can carry on accelerating. About 30 seconds after setting off, it can hit its top speed of 386 kmph (240 mph). That's a similar top speed to a **Formula 1** racing car and almost as fast as a US Champ Car, the world's fastest **circuit racing** car!

F1 VERSUS F1
Amazingly, test drives have shown that the McLaren F1 can actually accelerate faster than a Formula 1 racing car from 240 kmph (150 mph) to 270 kmph (170 mph). Its designers were able to give it such a stunning **performance** because they didn't have to stick to any of the rules that the designers of Formula 1 racing cars have to obey.

DRIVER OR PILOT?

The F1's seats are laid out in a unique way. Most sports cars have two seats, side by side. The F1's driver sits in the middle of the car, like a fighter pilot or the driver of a single-seat racing car. The seat is moulded to the driver's body, just like the seat of a Formula 1 racing car. Two passenger seats are fitted behind the driver's seat.

LIGHT WORK

Saving weight was so important to the McLaren F1's performance that every part was cut down as much as possible to save a few more kilograms. Even its hi-fi was specially designed so that it was half the weight of a normal car hi-fi. The tools supplied with most cars are normally made from steel, but the F1's toolkit is made from lighter **titanium** to save a bit more weight.

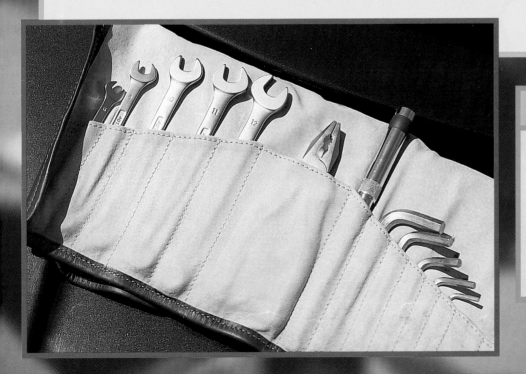

McLaren F1

Engine size: 6.1-litre V12

Engine power: 627 hp

Length: 4.3 metres

Weight: 1140 kg

Top speed: 386 kmph (240 mph)

Seats: 3

ENGINE POWER

Sports cars are powered by the same sort of engines as most family cars. All engines are designed to release energy from fuel and use it to turn the car's wheels. However, sports car engines generally have higher **performance**.

Sports car engines have between four and twelve **cylinders**. Each cylinder is a tube with a close-fitting **piston** that slides up and down inside it. **Fuel** is sprayed into each cylinder in turn, squashed by the piston and **ignited** by an electric spark. The burning fuel produces hot gases that expand and push the piston back down the cylinder. The up-and-down movements of all the pistons are changed into a spinning motion that drives the car's wheels. Bigger cylinders hold more fuel and air, so a bigger engine is usually more powerful than a small engine. But bigger engines are also heavier. To keep a sports car light, its designers generally fit it with a small engine. However, the engine can't be too small or it will lack the necessary power. The designer has to balance power against weight to get the required performance.

The serial 4 engine in a Toyota MR2.

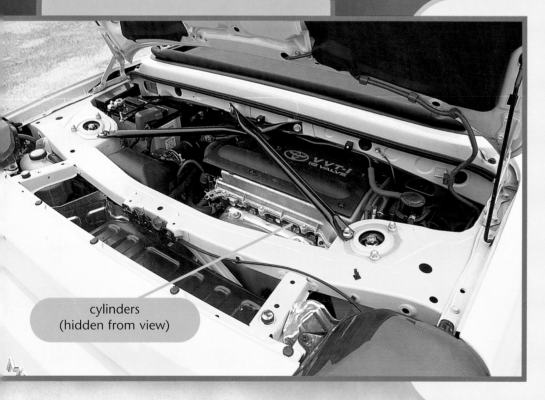

cylinders
(hidden from view)

LINES AND VEES

The Toyota MR2 sports car is powered by a four-cylinder engine. The cylinders stand upright in a row. It's called a **serial**, or in-line, engine. If a sports car designer wants to use a bigger engine with more than about six cylinders, there is not enough room to fit them in one long row. One answer is to have two rows, side by side. Usually, the two rows are arranged in a V shape. The eight-cylinder **V8** is a very popular sports car engine.

FLAT ENGINES

The Porsche Boxster uses another type of engine, called a flat 6. Its cylinders neither stand upright nor lean over to make a V shape. They lie flat. Imagine three bottles lying on their side next to each other. Now add a second row of three bottles bottom-to-bottom with the first row. That's how the cylinders are laid out in a flat 6 engine. With the cylinders lying flat, the weight of the engine is carried low, making the car more stable.

cylinders (x3)
– hidden from view

This illustration shows the combination of toothed wheels and shafts used to produce first and fourth gears.

First gear

from engine

to wheels

shafts

Fourth gear

from engine

to wheels

shafts

A BOX OF TEETH!

A sports car engine turns a set of toothed wheels in the **gearbox**. The gearbox is connected, through **shafts**, to the car's wheels. The driver chooses which **gear** to use. By changing gear, the driver can make the engine drive the car's wheels at anything from walking pace to its top speed.

Porsche Boxster S

Engine size: 3.2-litre flat 6

Engine power: 260 hp

Length: 4.32 metres

Weight: 1295 kg

Top speed: 264 kmph (164 mph)

Seats: 2

MUSCLE CARS

Some high-**performance** cars owe their **acceleration** and speed to an enormous engine under the bonnet.

The smallest city cars have an engine less than 1 litre in size. That's smaller than some motorcycle engines! An engine this size produces as little as 50 **horsepower**. A small sports car is driven by an engine roughly twice this size and power. A **Formula 1** racing car is powered by a 3-litre engine. But this is small compared to muscle cars. They are powered by engines of five litres or more – sometimes a lot more! These big-engine chargers include the USA's Chevrolet Corvette and Ford Mustang, but the classic muscle car is the Chrysler Viper. Its driver sits behind a massive 8-litre, 450-horsepower engine. No wonder the car has such a long bonnet!

AMERICA'S WILD HORSE

The US Ford Mustang is the most famous car in the USA and also the USA's best-selling muscle car. It was designed in the early 1960s to appeal to a new generation of young motorists looking for a more exciting drive. Since then, it has been redesigned and updated year after year. Today, with a 4.6-litre **V8** engine growling in front of the driver, the Mustang can reach 100 kmph (60 mph) in less than 5 seconds and reach a top speed of more than 250 kmph (155 mph).

The Viper GTS/R prototype on display in January 2000.

HIGHWAY SNAKE

The Chrysler Viper (Dodge Viper in the USA) started life as a 'concept car'. Concept cars show what designers think future cars might look like. Many of them are never manufactured, but so many people liked the Viper concept that Chrysler decided to build it. Its huge engine was developed from a truck engine. Its body was carefully designed to look good and also to remain stable at high speeds.

Chrysler Viper

Engine size: 8.0-litre V10
Engine power: 450 hp
Length: 4.5 metres
Weight: 1590 kg
Top speed: 309 kmph (192 mph)
Seats: 2

The original Chevrolet Corvette (pictured here) was the first US sports car. It went on sale in 1953.

A US FAVOURITE

The Corvette ZR-1 was a true supercar. Its rumbling 5.7-litre V8 engine soon made it the USA's favourite muscle car when it went on sale in 1989. The huge 340-horsepower engine can launch the 1.5-tonne car from a standing start to 100 kmph (60 mph) in only 4.5 seconds.

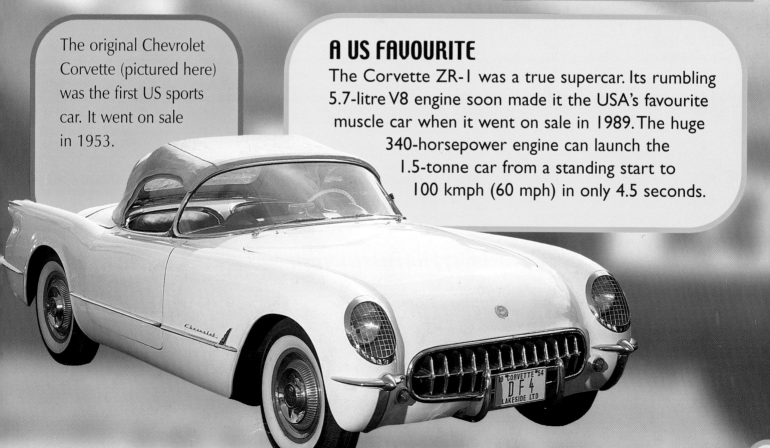

SMOOTH BODIES

The shape of a sports car affects its **acceleration**, top speed and **handling**. Designing the right shape improves its **performance**.

When a sports car moves, it has to push the air out of the way. Some of the engine's power is wasted in overcoming this air resistance, or **drag**. Different shapes cause different amounts of drag. A smooth body is better, because no parts stick out to catch the air rushing past the car. Some sports cars have their engine behind the driver. This lets the designer lower the front of the car and so reduce the drag it produces. However, designing a sports car is as much about making the car fun to drive as it is about producing a perfect design. A traditional sports car has an engine at the front and an open top. This isn't the fastest shape, but it's great fun to drive.

	Shape	Drag coefficient		Shape	Drag coefficient
air		0.04	air		0.80
air		0.42	air		0.82
air		0.47	air		1.05
air		0.50	air		1.15

This diagram shows the different coefficient of drag numbers produced by a selection of different shapes. The shapes with the smallest number give the least drag.

IT'S SUCH A DRAG!

The most **streamlined** sports cars are designed to create the least air resistance, or drag. The shape of the car is tested to find out how easily it slips through the air. The tests produce a number, called the coefficient of drag, which shows how 'slippery' the car is. The smaller the number, the more slippery it is. For a car the shape of a brick, the number is 1.0 or more. For a boxy family car, it is about 0.38. For very streamlined cars, like the Ferrari Enzo (pictured below), it is 0.30 or less.

COOL BODIES

Designing a car's body is made more complicated because it has to have holes in it. If the body was completely closed, the engine would be starved of air, and would overheat and break down. The engine needs air to burn its fuel and for cooling. The air enters the body through holes called ducts. They are carefully designed to let in the right amount of air without causing lots of drag.

A Ferrari Testarossa with air intake ducts on the sides.

SO SMOOTH

The Lamborghini Murciélago is one of the most streamlined cars ever made. Its headlights sit behind streamlined glass covers. Its wing mirrors are beautifully curved so that air slips around them. Its windows wrap around the car in line with the body. There are no bumps in the bodywork that might slow down the air flowing around the car.

Lamborghini Murciélago

Engine size: 6.2-litre V12
Engine power: 580 hp
Length: 4.58 metres
Weight: 1650 kg
Top speed: 330 kmph (205 mph)
Seats: 2

SUPERCARS

Supercars are the fastest and most expensive high-**performance** road cars. But only the wealthiest motorists can enjoy racing-car performance on the roads.

Sports cars are small and lightweight, but supercars are often heavier. They make up for their extra weight in two ways. First, they have a more powerful engine. Second, they are usually more **streamlined**. In 1985, the designers of the Lamborghini Diablo supercar were asked to produce the world's fastest **production car**. It would have to reach at least 320 kmph (200 mph) to beat the competition. The designers reduced its weight by using lighter materials and it was powered by the most powerful engine Lamborghini had built. It was indeed the fastest production car. And as we have seen, the designers at McLaren have also built a new type of supercar – the McLaren F1.

LAMBORGHINI DIABLO

The Lamborghini Diablo is a remarkable machine. Inside its elegant, swooping body, a huge, roaring six-litre engine sits behind the driver. The 550-**horsepower** engine can accelerate the 1.6-tonne car to about 325 kmph (205 mph). Acceleration is helped by the fact that most of the body parts, apart from the roof and the doors, are made from lightweight **carbon fibre**.

Lamborghini Diablo

Engine size: 6.0-litre V12
Engine power: 550 hp
Length: 4.47 metres
Weight: 1625 kg
Top speed: 325 kmph (205 mph)
Seats: 2

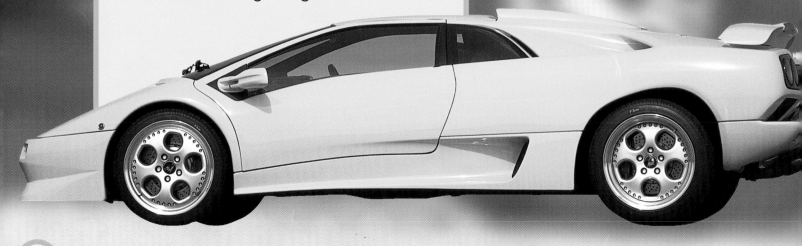

JAGUAR XJ220

When the Jaguar XJ220 was designed, it was to be powered by Jaguar's 5.3-litre **V12** engine. However, before the car was built, this was replaced by a modified 3.5-litre V6 racing engine. The racing engine was more powerful. It gave the new car a top speed of more than 340 kmph (210 mph) and made it the fastest production car ever built at the time (1992). Jaguar announced that it would make only 350 XJ220s. Within a few days, it had received over 1200 orders!

FERRARI F40

Ferrari's F40 was designed specially to celebrate the Italian car-maker's 40th anniversary. It was based on an earlier Ferrari, the 288 GTO, which had been developed for motor racing. The F40 was given a much lighter body made from carbon fibre instead of steel. Inside, the car was quite bare, adding to the feeling that it was a road-going racing car.

Modern sports cars are designed to be safe. If the worst happens and a sports car is involved in an accident, it is designed to protect the people inside it.

When a car hits something, it stops incredibly suddenly. Our soft bodies are easily damaged by the violent forces in a collision. Some of a sports car's safety features are designed to let the occupants come to a halt a little less suddenly. The seats, doors and **dashboard** are padded. Seatbelts hold the occupants safely in their seats and stop them from being hurled out through the windscreen. However, a seatbelt does not hold the head. It can fly forwards, causing neck injuries, and the driver's head may hit the steering wheel. To prevent this, cars are now often fitted with airbags that inflate and cushion the head in the event of an accident.

BELT UP!

Seat belts normally allow a driver or passenger to move around freely. But when a car hits something, the belt locks and stops the person wearing it from travelling forwards. Some sports cars are fitted with an extra safety feature called a pre-tensioner. In a collision, the seat belt doesn't just lock, it actually tightens and pulls the driver or passenger back into the seat.

SAFETY BAGS

When a car hits something, **sensors** detect the sudden stop and trigger the airbags. An **igniter** sets off a gas capsule that blows up the bag like a balloon. All of this happens within a fraction of a second. It has to be that quick to catch the driver's head before it hits the steering wheel.

ROCK AND ROLL

Convertible or open-top sports cars often have a thick bar that loops up behind the seats, above the driver's head. This is a roll bar and it has a life-saving purpose. If the car turns over, it supports the weight of the car and stops it from crushing the occupants underneath. Some cars that seem to have no roll bar have a very strong windscreen frame that does the same job.

The Ferarri 360 Spider has an individual roll bar for each seat.

CRASH TEST DUMMIES

All new car designs are tested by deliberately crashing them to make sure that they meet international safety regulations. Inside the car are life-size dummies designed to resemble a human driver and passengers. They weigh the same as people and they have joints in all the right places. They are also fitted with instruments to record the forces that act on them during a crash.

FUN CARS

A handful of sports cars are designed to be totally impractical for anything but having fun. They're designed and built for drivers to enjoy driving. Most of them look very basic indeed. They seem little more than an engine, a seat and four wheels. Because they are so basic, they are also amazingly light.

The tiny Caterham 7, for example, is more powerful than the 3.8-litre Ford Mustang muscle car, but is less than one third the weight of the mighty Mustang. This combination of more power and less weight produces neck-snappingly fast **acceleration**, sharper turning and higher speeds. The fastest Caterham 7 model, the Superlight R500, can get from zero to 100 kmph (60 mph) in 3.4 seconds, compared to 9.3 seconds for the Mustang.

CATERHAM 7

The Caterham 7 is designed to give its drivers a thrilling and exciting ride. It's an open-topped ultra-lightweight car. There are several different models powered by different engines. Some of them even use engines from high-performance motorcycles. The cars weigh about 500 kg. That's less than one third of the weight of a Ford Mustang.

Caterham 7 Superlight R500

Engine size: 1.8-litre serial 4
Engine power: 230 hp
Length: 3.38 metres
Weight: 460 kg
Top speed: 240 kmph (150 mph)
Seats: 2

ON THE PROWL

The Chrysler Prowler is designed to look dramatic and turn heads in the street. Its styling was inspired by cars called hot rods, built by car enthusiasts in the USA. Some hot rods are built for racing. Others are built for show. They're often built to look like old-fashioned family cars, but under their outer bodies they have a very powerful engine. The interior is often luxurious, with leather seats and a super sound system. The fun shape and extra weight of the hi-fi, luxurious interior and other additions affect the car's **performance**.

The designer of the Chrysler Prowler had to balance appearance and 'street-cred' against performance, **handling** and speed.

ATOM POWER

The British Ariel Atom looks like a metal skeleton on wheels. It has no doors, no windscreen and no roof. There is nowhere to store luggage. It certainly isn't **streamlined** either. And yet it is very fast – its top speed is 250 kmph (155 mph). Its secret is that it is a whopping 155 kilograms lighter than the ultra-light Lotus Elise sports car and has 60 more **horsepower** than the Elise.

DATA FILES

Every sports car is designed with a particular type of driver in mind. This table compares the basic specifications of some of today's best-known sports cars.

Car	Engine	Weight (kilograms)	Top speed (kmph / mph)	Time (seconds) 0–100 kmph (0–60 mph)
Ariel Atom 190	1.8-litre serial 4	600	250 / 155	unknown
BMW Z3	3.0-litre serial 6	1360	240 / 150	6.0
Chevrolet Corvette	5.7-litre V8	1455	280 / 175	4.5
Chrysler Prowler	3.5-litre V6	1295	210 / 130	6.5
Chrysler Viper	8.0-litre V10	1590	309 / 192	4.5
Ferrari Enzo	6.0-litre V12	1370	350 / 220	3.7
Ferrari F50	4.7-litre V12	1230	320 / 200	3.7
Ford Mustang	4.6-litre V8	1662	250 / 155	4.5
Jaguar XJ220	3.5-litre V6	1375	350 / 220	3.8
Lamborghini Diablo	6.0-litre V12	1625	325 / 205	3.8
Lotus 340R	1.8-litre serial 4	675	210 / 130	4.6
Lotus Elise	1.8-litre serial 4	755	200 / 125	5.7
Mazda MX-5	1.8-litre serial 4	1065	205 / 130	8.4
McLaren F1	6.1-litre V12	1140	386 / 240	3.2
Mercedes-Benz SLK 32 AMG	3.2-litre V6	1495	250 / 155	5.2
Porsche 911 GT3	3.6-litre flat 6	1350	300 / 185	4.8
Porsche Boxster	3.2-litre flat 6	1295	264 / 164	5.9
Toyota MR2	1.8-litre serial 4	960	210 / 130	7.9

JAGUAR'S E-TYPE

In the 1960s, one of the most famous sports cars in the world was the Jaguar E-type. Originally the E-type was designed as a racing car. However, when Jaguar pulled out of motor racing, the E-type was redesigned as a road car. A 1961 model with a 3.8-litre engine could 240 kmph (150 mph).

FURTHER READING AND RESEARCH

BOOKS AND MAGAZINES

Daily Express World Car Guide 2003
Every year, the *Daily Express* newspaper publishes a guide to the world's cars, with photographs of, and information about, hundreds of different models.

Century of Sports Cars, by Derek Avery, Caxton Editions, 1999
Supercars, by John Lamm, Motorbooks International, 2001

WEBSITES

http://www.howstuffworks.com
A website with simple explanations for how lots of things work, including engines and other parts of cars.

http://www.ukcar.com
A website with a 'how it works' section containing simple explanations for how things like seat belts and airbags work.

http://www.beaulieu.co.uk
The website of the National Motor Museum in England.

http://www.carsofthestars.com
Cars driven by the stars, including some of the high-performance cars driven by James Bond.

FERRARI'S 'RED HEAD'

Sports cars became very popular in the 1950s. Ferrari built one of its famous sports cars, the Testarossa, in 1956. It was called Testarossa (Italian for 'red head') after the red covers on top of the engine. It was a racing sports car and it was very successful indeed. Its 300-**horsepower**, 3-litre **V12** engine and lightweight **alloy** body gave it a top speed of about 270 kmph (170 mph).

GLOSSARY

accelerate go faster – a driver accelerates by pressing the accelerator pedal

air pressure pushing effect of air pressing against a surface

alloy metal made from a mixture of two or more different metals

aluminium lightweight metal that is easy to bend and shape

carbon fibre strong and lightweight material made from strands of carbon embedded in hard plastic

chassis frame on which a vehicle is built

circuit racing motor racing around a specially-built race-track

cylinder a tube-shaped part of a car engine where the fuel is burned. A sports car may have between four and twelve cylinders.

dashboard another name for a car's instrument panel

disc brakes brakes made of a disc (attached to a vehicle's wheel) between two tough pads. The disc spins with the wheel. When the driver presses the brake pedal, the pads grip the disc and slow it down.

downforce a force that presses a car down onto the road. It can be produced by a wing or by the shape of the car itself. Downforce helps a car to corner faster without skidding, because its tyres grip the ground better.

drag resistance to a car's movement through the air, caused by the air itself. As a car moves forwards, it has to push the air out of the way and the air pushes back. Drag is also called air resistance.

exhaust gases that rush out of an engine after the fuel has been burned

Formula 1 leading international motor racing championship

fuel a substance that is burned to produce power. Sports cars' engines burn petrol, a liquid made from oil.

gear a wheel with teeth around its edge. When two gear wheels are put together so that their teeth interlock, turning one wheel makes the other wheel turn too. If the wheels are the same size, they turn at the same speed. If one wheel is much bigger or smaller than the other, the wheels turn at different speeds.

gearbox set of gear wheels of different sizes. By linking different gear wheels so that their teeth lock together, the engine can be made to turn the car's wheels at a much wider range of speeds. Selecting different gear wheels like this is also called 'changing gear'.

GRP (Glass Reinforced Plastic) a material often used in car construction. GRP is made from glass fibres embedded in plastic. It is easily moulded into the shape of a car's body. Some sports cars have a GRP body because GRP is lighter than metal.

handling way a car responds or reacts when it is being driven, and how well it holds the road

horsepower (hp) measurement showing how much work an engine can do

ignite set on fire – the fuel inside an engine is set on fire by an electric spark

manoeuvrable steerable. A more manoeuvrable car can make tighter turns than most other cars.

performance capabilities. A high-performance car is capable of faster acceleration and higher speeds than most cars.

piston the part of a car's engine that slides back and forth inside the cylinder where the fuel is burned. Each time the fuel is burned, the piston is pushed down the cylinder. The back and forth movements turn the car's wheels.

production car car built in large numbers for sale

replica precise copy. A replica car is a modern copy of an older model.

road-holding a car's ability to grip the road without skidding, especially as it turns corners

sensors devices that take measurements. Sensors measure everything from engine temperature to oil pressure. They are connected to the instruments in front of the driver and to the car's computer, if it has one.

serial engine type of engine that has a number of cylinders in a row

shaft revolving rod. Shafts are used in cars to transmit motion or power from one place to another, from the engine to the wheels for example.

spoiler a panel or strip fitted to a car to produce downforce or stop the car from taking off like a plane when it goes very fast

streamlined designed to move through air very easily, producing very little air resistance. Smooth, gently curving shapes are more streamlined than rough or boxy shapes. A fish's body is one of the most streamlined shapes.

titanium strong, lightweight metal that is used to make some car parts instead of steel. Titanium does not rust, as steel does, and it can withstand very high temperatures. Unfortunately, it is also very expensive.

V6, V8, V12 type of car engine with six, eight or twelve cylinders. The cylinders are arranged in two rows, or banks. The two rows of cylinders spin a shaft that runs along the bottom of the engine. The cylinders lean outwards from this shaft, giving the engine its V shape. The number after the 'V' shows how many cylinders the engine has.

wind tunnel large pipe that air is blown through, used for testing how cars and other vehicles behave at different speeds. Instead of being driven through the air, the car stays still and the air is blown at the car. Small models of cars are often used, but some wind tunnels are big enough for full-size cars.

INDEX

East
DUMBARTONSHIRE